OR TODAY'S NEEDS

Messages that speak from the caring heart of God to the hurting human heart.

God's Comfort

Constance Vanides

A Potter's Press **Tear-Apart**™ Book

The Potter's Press — Palos Verdes Peninsula, California

Cover design: Steve Vanides, Chicago, Illinois.

GOD'S COMFORT FOR TODAY'S NEEDS.

Copyright © 1986, 1987 by Constance Vanides.

Printed and bound in the United States of America. Permission is given to copy individual messages for the purposes of personal Christian ministry. Reproducing the material in this book for resale is not permitted.

Published by The Potter's Press, P.O. Box 7000-150, Palos Verdes Peninsula, California 90274.

ISBN 0-9617465-0-5

How To Use This Book

Give as a gift: Here is the book you've been waiting for! It's a selection of God's messages for that person who needs to hear of God's power today to make him/her whole, to comfort and assure the hurting one of His abiding presence, to bring abundant life to those without hope. You can give a gift of God's love to the lonely, rejected and unloved and a ray of sunshine from one who does care — you!

Share individually with others: These timely messages of God's words of comfort are printed on perforated Tear-Apart™ pages. This allows the messages to be removed and shared directly with others, an expression of your caring with someone who has a need to know God's concern and encouragement for a particular time.

Frame a single page: If one message is particularly meaningful, it can easily be removed from this Tear-Apart™ book. Frame the message and hang it up, or give as a gift.

Reproduce individual messages: Permission is given to copy and give away pages as your Christian ministry leads you.

Use as a devotional: for private meditation time or share in prayer, small groups or church gatherings. A topical index at the back of this book will help you to locate the appropriate message.

Whatever way they are used, these are God's words and we have His promise that His word will not return to Him void.

To God be the glory!

Contents

Preface 9

Called From The Beginning 13
Look To My Face 15
Light Of Life 17
Care For The Little Ones 19
Look To The Light 21
My New Creature 23
My Love Sustains 25
Give Me All 27
Yours To Take 29
Abundant Life 31
I Meet Your Needs 33
Treasures Of Heaven 35
Comfort In Need 37
I Have Made You Clean 39
I Will Sustain You 41
One With The Father 43
Come, Consenting Heart 45
I Lead My Own 47
The Joyful Life 49
Alive In You 51
You Are My Light 53
Always With Me 55
My Life Is For You 57
Courage 59
Know My Voice 61

Contents

Worship	63
Of Single Purpose	65
I Would Lead You Forward	67
My Fullness In You	69
Christos Anesti	71
My Yoke Is Easy	73
He Is With Me	75
All Things New	77
Wait Upon Me	79
Let Me Enfold You	81
The Silent Message	83
The Past Is Gone	85
Seek Me And Trust	87
With You Forever	89
Time Of Refreshment	91
Willingness To Believe	93
I Make You Free	95
I Seek My Own	97
I Run Beside You	99
Wisdom Revealed	101
I Am Your Victory	103
All Things Are Possible	105
A New Love	107
Topical Index	109

Preface

These messages from God were given to me to share, that they may comfort those in need.

They are not my words. I am awakened from sleep in early morning hours with a sentence and the urging to get up and write it down. As I am obedient to this calling and write the words on paper, the next sentence comes. Without any conscious thinking on my part, the entire message is given, often as fast as I can write.

These words are meant to be shared. That is why they are printed on perforated paper. You may tear them out, and pass them on to a friend in need or frame them and give them as a gift. Or you may wish to copy any one of them and include it in a note or card to encourage someone in a time of trial.

Although they have been copyrighted, you have my permission to reproduce an individual message if it is for the purpose of Christian ministry and not for resale. Share these messages as you are led, perhaps with a prayer partner, or read aloud as a devotional to a group. You will find as I have, that if this is done prayerfully, and with the love you have in your heart for those who are hurting, people will be strengthened, knowing God truly continues to protect and care for His children.

I only ask that you give credit to the Almighty Father, to Jesus, His Son, who died for us, and to the Holy Spirit, who guides and encourages, comforting us always with His presence.

Constance Vanides

God's Comfort

For Today's Needs

Called from the Beginning

Why call Me
to be by your side
when I am always near?
Know you not that
I have called you
from the beginning
to be my own?
My grace alone has held
you to Me.

Look to My Face

Ask Me not the why or wherefore.
Cast aside all carnal questionings.
Do not even try to reason
or to judge those motives not of Me.
Cease now, desist, be still.
It is enough that you know Me.
Look only to My face.
Know My comfort is in you.
Rest then, in peace surrender
your mind at one with Mine divine!

Light of Life

Fear not the thoughts
that from the darkness come.
Look only to Me.
For in Me there is no dark at all.
I am the only light,
the light of all the world.
There can be no darkness
when I am in you.
Cast away all evil in My name
and it will flee from you.
Think on the things only I can give.
The pure things of the world,
the beautiful and undefiled,
these are Mine and the bright light of life.

Care for the Little Ones

Care for the little ones.
For I have placed them on the earth
each for My own purposes.
Each one I call to be My own,
to him will I give
the desire to know Me.
Each one do I love.
Each is created in My image
and will learn to seek Me first.
I need each one,
obedient to do My will
and to show My love.
So love each of My little ones.
These I've placed in your earthly care.
Teach them to know Me
and to follow in all My ways.

Look
to the Light

Look only to Me.
For I am the light of the world.
When your eye perceives Me
your whole body is light.
Seeing evil only
will bring about the darkness.

My New Creature

I see not your imperfections.
I see only the heart
given willingly to Me.
All things are past, forgotten.
Today are all things made new.
You are My new creature,
made clean all over
with My glory shining in you!

My Love Sustains

Though the storms of life
are all around you,
yet will I be your protection.
No harm shall befall you.
Yea, though men fall
'round about you,
will I hold you.
With My right hand
will you be held up.
For you have heard My command
to follow Me,
and you have come,
forsaking others.
My love alone sustains
and is your strength.

Give Me All

Allow Me to be your strength,
to comfort and console you.
Look not to man for this
for I came to let you know
of this love I have for you.
I will never leave or forsake you.
Believe this now with all your heart.
Give Me your pains and sorrows,
all those thoughts that now torment you.
Give them all to Me
and I will give you peace.

Yours to Take

Fear not what man can do to you.
Trust only in My power and My might.
I only will sustain you.
I desire your closeness to Me
for I am a jealous God.
I long to give you so much.
Reach out, My children, and take.
What I give is Living Water,
that you may never thirst again.
Take, drink. All is for you
that My Father is glorified!
Continue in your praises of Me.
For in them I am living in you.

Abundant Life

Open My Book
and present yourself to Me.
Remove all distractions
from your way
and focus clearly on My Word.
For there is My life to be had:
all you can eat, all to drink.
To overflowing will I give
you who would search.
Ask that the veil be lifted
from your eyes
to diligently seek My face.
I will never disappoint,
but rather provide you with all things.

I Meet Your Needs

Determine to know nothing
but what I have for you.
Rest in quiet assurance
that your needs are being met.
Worry not. Be anxious for nothing.
All things are Mine,
and they are yours.
Your full trust is all I desire.
Then can I work
to meet your every need.
I know your heart's desire.
All I ask is your obedience
to the leading of the Holy Spirit.
Be in prayer. Worship and wait.

Treasures of Heaven

Rely only upon Me
and not on the riches of this world.
Treasures laid up on earth
will only fade and disappear,
but the treasures of Heaven
are for eternity.
My Word will never fade
neither will it be gone.
My truths are beyond
the world's understanding.
It is given only to those
whose minds are stayed on Me.
To these do I impart My spiritual truths
and the peace only I can give.

Comfort In Need

Quiet. Peace.
Those who believe in Me
rest in the assurance
of My promises.
They can rely on My presence
to comfort in times of need.
They have My strength in trials
beyond human endurance.
All that I am is for you
to appropriate as your own.
Come be My own,
that you may know
what fullness I have for you,
what joy there is yet to live!

I Have Made You Clean

My child, I hear your prayers of repentance
and I forgive. This is My nature.
For I am love.
In love created I you to have My mind,
so that you can do all things.
I am with you to do My pleasure.
For it is already in you—that desire to please Me.
Let no other thoughts be before you,
but look to Me as you have done
and continue in this way.
For I have made you clean.
Be assured in this.
I give you My peace.

I Will Sustain You

Take only what you can carry and follow Me.
For the day is coming when nothing else
will be necessary.
Only I will sustain you.
All the familiar will pass away.
Only My love will remain.
It remains in the hearts
of those who know Me.
Yes, My love is in you
and will sustain and carry you.

One With the Father

Marvel not that you
should be called the sons of God.
For whoever calls upon Me
becomes one with the Father.
Know you not that you are to enter
by the narrow gate to follow Me?
This is the only way to God.
I have prepared this for the one
who searches for the truth.
I am the truth, the way and the life.
Whoever follows Me shall not stumble
but shall have life everlasting.
Put aside all other thoughts.
My ways are not the ways
of the world.
My ways are love and peace
to the submitted heart.

Come, Consenting Heart

No shadow of turning with Me.
I am the same, yesterday, today
and forever. I change not.
Therefore, I say to you today
that I forgive repentant hearts
humbled before Me.
Awareness of sins brought before Me
I will take—for these have I already taken
by My blood that's been shed for you.
I wait only for the consenting heart
to come to Me, willing
to be made My own.

I Lead My Own

Look to Me only.
I am that light
that guides your way.
I am the truth
that leads you.
I have shown you
through My words
the way to go.
Through My word only
will you find true peace.
Concern yourself not
with those things
that you can do nothing about.
Rather leave them in My hands.
Given to Me, I can then work
to bring about the solution.
Trust that I can do this.
I will lead My own,
those who know My voice and follow.

The Joyful Life

I have given you all that I am.
Therefore, receive it.
It is for you, given that you
may have life abundantly.
Let no distractions deter you
from using these graces,
given freely to all who are Mine.
As you look more to Me
will you be able to live
the joyful life.
Rest, and be not anxious.
Each day's manna will be supplied.
Joy is My presence with and in you.

You Are My Light

My warmth surrounds you
in the midst of this wicked generation.
Walk in it and be glad
for I have put you here
as a light to shine in the darkness.
People will see you and know
that you are Mine
and will be drawn to you
to know the more of Me.
Do not fear, for I have sent angels
to protect you as you follow
what I would have you do.

Always With Me

You should have no thought for tomorrow.
I have provided for your life
throughout all eternity.
It is to be with Me.
All your loved ones will be with you,
including the unborn of every generation.
I only require your present life
to be lived fully in Me,
following My ways, My commands.
I have given you this desire
for you are one of Mine.
My sheep know My voice
and another they will not follow.
Once you strayed, but now have I found you
to be forever in My bosom.

My Life is for You

These things that I tell you now
are those things you know
from your heart.
My words never die
but are life and power
for the man who thirsts
and searches for something better.
Only want to ask,
and I give you all.
It only requires belief in My name,
and all I have and am is for you.

Courage

Courage. The word is courage
for what you are to endure.
But I will be with you all the way.
Have no fear, for I will give you strength.
Lean only on Me.
You may believe that
all I've said is now for you.
In the midst of trials,
My peace is with you—
yes, that peace that
the world cannot understand.
But you have become one with Me,
and I have overcome the world.
Keep your eyes on Me alone.
Look neither to the right nor left.
Focus only upon Me.
I will never leave you.

Know My Voice

I would that you only rest
in the love I have for you.
Rest your mind from thoughts
that take you away from Me.
Life in Me is so much more
than striving on your own can be.
Allow Me to be the source of life in you.
I am the Alpha and Omega.
Your life begins with Me.
And when it's lived in My fullness,
then your life ends, too, on earth
into My blessedness, forever with Me.
Again, there is nothing to fear
for I am with you, gently leading,
always guiding.
You need only to know My voice.

Worship

Come into My presence with singing!
Yes, sing a joyful song to Me.
A new song would I hear,
for I have put the song in your heart.
I have given you the words,
and now I can rejoice with you
as you come joyfully before Me.
For you have known Me
and My joy is in you.
Show that joy to Me in songs of praise,
of worship and adoration.
For as such is the Kingdom of Heaven,
the many voices singing of My glories.
"Glory, glory in the highest!"
"Worthy is the Lamb!"
"Sing alleluia, alleluia and amen!"
For I am the beginning and the end,
who is and was and ever shall be!

Of Single Purpose

The time of mourning is over.
Wipe away all tears
and turn not back.
Look only to what I have for you.
Keep your eyes on Me alone.
I will uphold you
with My right hand
and guide you to the next step.
Your eyes need to be of single purpose.
Praise Me in the ending.
Praise Me in the middle.
Praise Me for what is to come.
Pray for all, that My Spirit
will prepare each one in His time.
Leave behind all thoughts of criticism
and go forward in My might!

I Would Lead You Forward

The dark is not dark
for I am with you.
Be not afraid of the unknown.
I am there to guide you.
I turn on each light
as you step out to follow,
illuminating the way
one moment at a time.
You may rest briefly,
but turning back is surely grief
when I would lead you forward.
Pure trust is what I desire from you.
Then doubt's companion, fear,
is driven away,
making all things light for you
that you may see clearly
and not stumble.

My Fullness in You

I am with you
wherever you may go.
You have chosen to follow Me.
And so by your side
will I remain forever.
I was with you
when you first began on earth.
I will be with you
at the ending of your life
and beyond for all eternity.
For I have said that
I will never leave or forsake you.
Receive this, then,
and have no fear
for what tomorrow may bring.
My presence is your very strength.
You have no need for any other.
You have My fullness in you
now and forevermore.

Christos Anesti

I am risen!
I am no longer in the tomb.
Three days have I ministered
to those under the earth
and now they are set free.
And you, the living still,
have you chosen to live in Me,
that you may live and never die?
My resurrection is for you.
Today you may rise beyond
the bondages of the past.
You may rise with Me,
victorious in this life,
raised in glory in the next!
Christos Anesti!
Truly I have risen!

My Yoke is Easy

Come, unburden yourself before Me.
In My presence, give Me all your concerns.
For I have come to take all upon Me
as I lead you along the way.
See how easy now it is!
Continue only with Me.
I carry the heaviest load
and yours has become light.
Rejoice in this!
You need not carry it all yourself.
I am constantly at your side to relieve you.
Know this, and release that weight
upon Me now.

He is With Me

Would I have told you
if it were not so?
Truly, I have prepared a place
for you, for your loved ones,
that where I am you may be also.
For My Father's house has many rooms,
room enough for all who
yearn for My presence.
Trust Me for this
though your heart be troubled now.
Lay aside all earthly woes.
My Kingdom is not of this world.
It is more glorious
than you can ever imagine!
Wipe away those tears.
I gave My life that you
may no longer sorrow, nor weep.
Your loved one is with Me.

All Things New

I am doing a new thing in you.
Old ways are past.
The new is upon you now.
Only let Me be your guide.
Lay aside your own thoughts,
for you are My new creation.
Truly your old man has died.
I make all things new.

Wait Upon Me

Do not be concerned.
All things are in My hands.
I only require that you wait.
Wait for My leading
and I will make all to come to pass
as it shall be.
You are to be where I want you
and to know that I am there—
in every situation,
in all places, at all times.
Your attention is to be
directed only upon Me.
Then shall My glory be brought forth,
as the sun breaks through clouds of darkness.
Wait, wait upon Me.

Let Me Enfold You

Can you see yourself as My child?
Do you feel like a child in My presence?
Do you know what it is to have Me hold you
and care for you and love you?
I want you as a child,
forbidding those who would
keep you away from Me.
I long to have you with Me
so you would never fear again.
Come, as that child.
Come, and let Me enfold you
in the love only I can give.

The Silent Message

I would have you know Me in your heart.
In the quiet of your inner being
is where you shall know Me.
You need no other stimulus
but your deep desire to have Me in you.
You will not find this in a crowd.
But once found, your desire will be
to be with others in your praise of Me.
Until then, I would have you silent before Me,
submitted, allowing Me to minister
to your deepest need.
No action on your part is needful,
only your need to know Me,
My Spirit in yours!

The Past is Gone

Release the past into My hand, dear one.
That which was is never to be again.
I am making of you a new creation.
But I cannot do this without your release
of the things that hold you from before.
Do you not know what I have yet before you?
There's excitement in My presence
and wonders to behold as you walk with Me.
See this for you today, the joy and gladness
of your life in Mine!

Seek Me And Trust

I will let you know what you are to do.
Only come before Me in complete submission
and I will point the way.
Are you at a crossroads, dear one?
Are there choices you must make?
Are there important decisions
to be made right now?
All these and more I will take care of for you.
You need not be anxious,
filled with worry or with fear.
Each day placed in My hands
will be rewarded with,
not only solutions, but My peace as well.
See to it, My beloved, to clearly seek Me
and trust in Me to respond.

With You Forever

Do you not know I am always with you?
In the midst of sorrows
I am there to sustain, to comfort,
to give the life abundant.
Only reach out and I am there
with you forever by your side.
Your weakness is My strength.
In your need will I respond.
Truly, you are never alone.

Time of Refreshment

Put aside all other thoughts for now
and let your thoughts be only for Me,
for I have much to say to you.
Yet you will not listen in your present state.
Come into your quiet place so that I may speak
and you would listen.
My commands are not always for action
but are often that you would stop
and receive the time of refreshment from Me.
Let Me fill you with My presence,
My wisdom for the time at hand,
My love for dealing with those who trouble you.
Then can you return, knowing My words
will sustain and be your strength.
Come then, enter into My rest.

Willingness to Believe

I will take care of you. Have no fear.
I have held you in My arms
for all these years.
Will I not continue to be with you,
caring for you, loving you?

I Make You Free

Whom the son has made free is free indeed!
You find yourself free
when you become My servant.
Then you truly are freed
from the bondages of the world.
When you are freed to worship Me,
the things of earth no longer give stress.
For you know Me and in Me there is none of this;
only peace and joy in the Spirit.
Tribulation is of the world,
but I have overcome it all.
I have made you My own
and you were willing to come
and lay your life before Me.
My bondservant? Yours is the choice.
And so I make you free!

I Seek My Own

Enter into My courts with praise.
For I, the Lord am gracious,
full of compassion and am from everlasting.
Since I have been from the beginning
and will continue on through all eternity,
I continue to seek after My own.
Those whom I have called
do I wait for and desire them to know Me.
So join into praises of Me.
Surely it shall always be.

Alive in You

Alive! I am alive
in each believer's heart.
My presence in you
is to know the truth,
the truth that enables
the searching heart
to act in freedom.
With My mind in you
can you do all things
in the strength I alone can give.
Be not dismayed, afraid or anxious.
For each step of the way
do I lead you.
My outstretched hand
is always there,
ready for your reach.
It takes a humbleness on your part
to ask for help, to knock,
to reach out to Me.
This great faith will make you whole.

I Run Beside You

Run the good race
is what I've called you to do,
to go forward with all I've given you,
with the strength I give.
It is not your struggle alone,
the living of this life.
I run beside you.
Blessed is the man who sees Me at his side.
For I give what is needed.
The victor of the race receives a crown.
In the spiritual realm it's one of glory.
You, too, are glorified with Me
in My great heavenly realm.
You know the rules. Continue on!

Wisdom Revealed

All things are made plain in your sight
when you know Me.
All things will I show you.
Only trust that I will reveal them.
As you ask, will it be shown.
Those who deligently seek
will find the wisdom to know
the answer for each need.
Put Me first in your heart.
All other things will surely follow.

I Am Your Victory

Cast away your fears.
I have provided and cared for you
all these years.
Will I not continue to do so?
I am faithful and I never change.
Under My wings will you be protected
and kept from all harm.
So let not the thoughts
that Satan puts into your mind
take over and possess you.
He is the author of lies
and would destroy you
if you let him.
Again, look only to Me and what I am.
Your victory, your life is lived only in Me.
Give praise to My name.

All Things Are Possible

If I can? I surely can if you believe.
All things are possible if you believe.
If others have told you otherwise
and you've heard the voice of the deceiver,
it becomes a hard saying for you.
But if you come to Me pure as a little child,
then you are persuaded that with your heavenly
Father, all things are possible.
The need is to look only to Me.
See what I have done in the past
and continue to do today.
The most difficult cases I bring cures,
for this is to God's glory and to no other.
If I seem to delay along the way,
it brings the greater glory to God.
I require that persistency in prayer,
acknowledging My faithfulness in situations
deemed hopeless in yourself;
and a complete submission to Me.

A New Love

You are My beloved.
I have called you to Me since the very beginning.
Forsake those things that meant so much before
and come now to Me.
I alone can fill the emptiness you feel.
I alone give meaning to your life.
If you allow Me, I will fill your life with abundance,
that which only I can give. Yield to Me, My love.
I wait until you are willing
and are prepared to meet Me.
Turn from that which does not satisfy.
I give Living Water so you may never thirst,
daily manna that you may be filled,
and for your soul, fullness of joy.
I provide this for My own,
those who forsake the ways of man
and seek for and yearn to know their Creator God.
I will not disappoint.
I provide My care, preparing your way to know Me.
I resurrect from the ruins of your life
new life lived in Me.
Are you willing to surrender totally, dear one?

Topical Index

abundant life	49, 89, 107
always near	13, 37, 73, 79, 89
answers	101
anxious	33, 49, 51, 87
ask	51, 57, 101
assurance	37, 39
beginning	61, 63, 97, 107
belief, believe	27, 37, 57, 93, 105
beside you	99
bondages	71, 95
called you	13, 97, 107
care(d)	19, 31, 93, 103
carry, I will	41, 73
child, as a (My)	39, 81, 105
choices	87, 95
comfort	15, 27, 37, 89
compassion	97
consenting heart	23, 45
courage	59
created in My image	19
criticism	65
dark(ness)	17, 21, 53, 67, 79
deceiver	103, 105
decisions	87
delay	105
desire to please	39
disappoint	31, 107
distractions	31, 49
doubt	67
emptiness	107
eternal, eternity, everlasting	35, 43, 55, 63, 69, 97
evil	17, 21
faithfulness, My	103, 105
faith	51
fear(s)	17, 29, 53, 59, 61, 67, 69, 81, 87, 93, 103
follow Me	19, 25, 41, 43, 47, 53, 55, 67, 69
forgiveness	39, 45
forgotten	23
forward	65, 67, 99
freely given	49
free(dom)	51, 71, 95
fullness in you, My	37, 55, 61, 69, 107
glory, glorious	23, 63, 71, 75, 79, 99, 105
grace(s), gracious	13, 49, 97
guide(ing)	61, 65, 67, 77
heart's desire	33
humbleness	45, 51
imperfections	23
joy, (ful)	37, 49, 63, 85, 95, 107
Kingdom	63, 75
know Me (My voice)	15, 19, 41, 53, 61, 63, 83, 97, 101, 107
leading	61, 65, 67, 73, 77, 79
life and power	57
life everlasting	43, 71
life in Me	61, 71, 85, 103
light of life	17
light of the world	17, 21
light that guides	47, 67
light to shine	53
listen	91
little ones	19
Living Water	29, 107
look to Me	15, 17, 21, 39, 47, 49, 59, 65, 79, 103, 105
love	19, 25, 27, 39, 41, 43, 61, 81, 91, 93
make you whole	51
many rooms	75
meaning to life	107

Topical Index (Cont'd)

mind in you, My	39, 51
mourning	65
need	33, 37, 69, 89
never alone	89, 99
never leave you	27, 59, 69
new life (creation)	23, 77, 85, 107
no thought for tomorrow	55
obedience	19, 33
one mind	15
one of Mine	19, 55
one with Me	59
overflowing	31
pains	27
past	71, 77, 85
peace	15, 27, 35, 37, 39, 43, 47, 59, 87, 95
praise	29, 63, 65, 83, 97, 103
pray, prayer(s)	33, 39, 65, 105
promises	27, 31, 37
protection	25, 53, 93, 103
provide(d), provision	31, 33, 55, 103, 107
questionings	15
quiet	15, 33, 37, 83, 91
race	99
reach out	29, 51, 89
refreshment	91
rejoice	63, 73
release	43, 73, 85
rely on Me	35, 37
repentance	39, 45
respond	89
rest	15, 33, 37, 49, 61, 67, 91
resurrection life	71, 107
risen	71
seek Me	19, 31, 87
seek truth	43, 101
servant	95
sing(ing) song	63
solutions	47, 87
sorrow(s)	25, 27, 75, 89
source of life	61
Spirit	33, 65, 83, 95
strength	25, 27, 37, 51, 59, 69, 89, 91, 99
stress	95
submission	15, 43, 83, 87, 105
surrender	15, 107
sustain, I will	25, 29, 41, 89, 91
tears	65, 75
thought(s)	17, 27, 39, 55, 61, 77, 91, 103
treasures of heaven	35
trials, tribulations	25, 37, 59, 75, 95
trouble(s)	25, 27, 75, 91
trust	29, 33, 47, 67, 75, 87, 101
truth(s)	35, 43, 47, 51
turn not back	65
uphold	25, 65, 73
victor(y), (ious)	71, 99, 103
wait	33, 79
weakness	89
whole	51
willing (heart)	23, 45, 95, 107
wisdom	91, 101
with Me	55, 75, 81, 85
with you	59, 69, 79, 89
word(s), My	31, 35, 47, 57, 91
worry	33, 87
worship	33, 63, 95

God's Comfort For Today's Needs

We welcome your comments and/or suggestions.

Please circle the following Yes or No:

- Was this book purchased for yourself? Yes No
- Did you receive this book as a gift? Yes No
- Do you intend to tear-apart the pages? Yes No
- Have you shared the messages? Yes No
  If yes, how were they shared?
      With a group? Yes No
      With individuals? Yes No
      Reproduced a message? Yes No
      Gave a Tear-Apart™ page? Yes No
      Tape recorded readings? Yes No
      Other _____

- Would you purchase additional volumes with messages that are uplifting and/or exhorting? Yes No

Additional Comments: _____

_____

_____

_____

(please check)
Mr.____ Mrs.____ Ms.____ Miss____ Dr.____ Rev.____

First Name_____ Last Name_____

Address: _____

City _____ State ____ Zip ____

The Potter's Press
P.O. Box 7000-150
Palos Verdes Peninsula, CA
90274-0299

(Fold on dotted line and tape)

first
class
stamp

The Potter's Press
P.O. Box 7000-150
Palos Verdes Peninsula, CA 90274-0299

the Potter's Press
P.O. Box 1314
Vacaville, CA 95696